Timeline

BOOK OF CENTURIES

This book belongs to:

....

If found, please contact me at:

....

Dear Fellow Student,

This book is your own blank timeline book. Books like these have been used by students of all ages--elementary school students, middle school students, high school students, university students, and even adults who are life-long learners. You can make fascinating connections by jotting down the interesting things you learn in history, science, literature, music, art, and other subjects.

Enjoy this book, try to write neatly, but don't worry about it being perfect. As the years pass, you'll find this book becomes one of your most treasured keepsakes. Best wishes on your studies.

C. Whitney

P.S. I value your insight and would appreciate if you would leave a review. Thank you and enjoy!

Timeline Book of Centuries: The Details

- **Paperback** - more portable than a wall timeline
- **See each century at a glance** - two-page spread for each century from 4000 BC to AD 2100
- **Organized** - each century has rows to record People, Wars & Events, Discoveries, Literature, Music, Art
- **Space to record earliest history** - starts with undated two-page spread for earliest history
- **Extra pages** - lined and unlined pages in the back of the book for notes, lists, and drawings
- **Large 8.5 inch. x 11 inch pages** - plenty of room to write entries

	AD 1801-1825	AD 1826-1850
PEOPLE	1803-1806 Louisiana Purchase and Lewis + Clark expedition	
WARS & EVENTS		1848-1855 *California goldrush*
DISCOVERIES	1804 Steam locomotive	1829 Louis Braille invents braille
LITERATURE	1812 First edition of Grimm's Fairy Tales	1830-1890 *Romantic* Period
MUSIC		
ART	**WILLIAM BLAKE** The Horse, 1805	**J.M.W. TUR** The Harb Dieppe,

PEOPLE

...oln U.S. President 🎩

...marck unifies Germany

WARS & EVENTS

...american Civil War

1898 Spanish-American War

...nada established 🍁

DISCOVERIES

1876 Alexander Graham Bell
invents, patents telephone

LITERATURE

Moby Dick-Herman Melville 🐋

1884 Huckleberry Finn-Mark Twain

MUSIC

1893 Antonin Dvorak (Czech)
New World Symphony

...875 Tchaikovsky (Russian) 💃
Swan Lake Ballet

ART

CLAUDE MONET

Poppies in a
Field, 1873

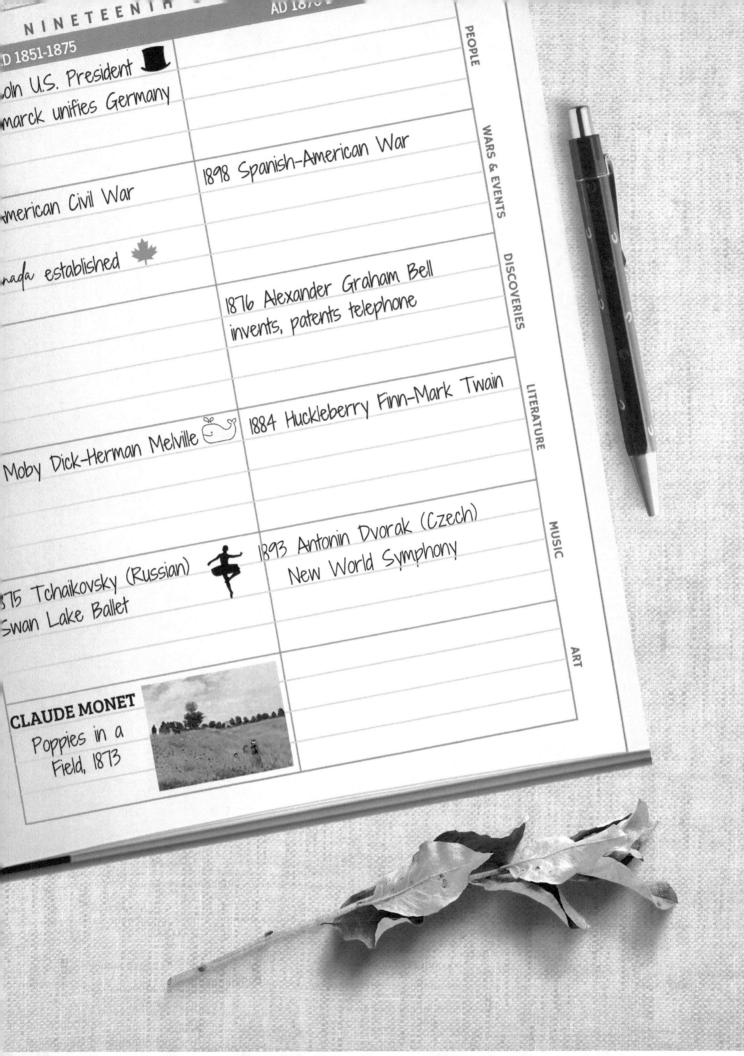

History is the witness
that testifies to the passing of time;
it illumines reality,
vitalizes memory,
provides guidance in daily life,
and brings us tidings of antiquities.

———

MARCUS TULLIUS CICERO

PEOPLE		
WARS & EVENTS		
DISCOVERIES		
LITERATURE		
MUSIC		
ART		

EARLIEST HISTORY

PEOPLE

WARS & EVENTS

DISCOVERIES

LITERATURE

MUSIC

ART

FORTIETH CENTURY BC

	4000-3976 BC	3975-3951 BC
PEOPLE		
WARS & EVENTS		
DISCOVERIES		
LITERATURE		
MUSIC		
ART		

FORTIETH CENTURY BC

3950-3926 BC	3925-3901 BC	
		PEOPLE
		WARS & EVENTS
		DISCOVERIES
		LITERATURE
		MUSIC
		ART

3900-3876 BC	3875-3851 BC

PEOPLE

WARS & EVENTS

DISCOVERIES

LITERATURE

MUSIC

ART

3900-3876 BC	3875-3851 BC

3850-3826 BC	3825-3801 BC	
		PEOPLE
		WARS & EVENTS
		DISCOVERIES
		LITERATURE
		MUSIC
		ART

THIRTY-EIGHTH CENTURY BC

	3800-3776 BC	3775-3751 BC
PEOPLE		
WARS & EVENTS		
DISCOVERIES		
LITERATURE		
MUSIC		
ART		

	3800-3776 BC	3775-3751 BC

3750-3726 BC	3725-3701 BC	
		PEOPLE
		WARS & EVENTS
		DISCOVERIES
		LITERATURE
		MUSIC
		ART

	3700-3676 BC	3675-3651 BC
PEOPLE		
WARS & EVENTS		
DISCOVERIES		
LITERATURE		
MUSIC		
ART		

THIRTY-SEVENTH CENTURY BC

3650-3626 BC	3625-3601 BC	
		PEOPLE
		WARS & EVENTS
		DISCOVERIES
		LITERATURE
		MUSIC
		ART

THIRTY-SIXTH CENTURY BC

	3600-3576 BC	3575-3551 BC
PEOPLE		
WARS & EVENTS		
DISCOVERIES		
LITERATURE		
MUSIC		
ART		

THIRTY-SIXTH CENTURY BC

3550-3526 BC	3525-3501 BC	
		PEOPLE
		WARS & EVENTS
		DISCOVERIES
		LITERATURE
		MUSIC
		ART

THIRTY-FIFTH CENTURY BC

	3500-3476 BC	3475-3451 BC
PEOPLE		
WARS & EVENTS		
DISCOVERIES		
LITERATURE		
MUSIC		
ART		

THIRTY-FIFTH CENTURY BC

3450-3426 BC	3425-3401 BC	
		PEOPLE
		WARS & EVENTS
		DISCOVERIES
		LITERATURE
		MUSIC
		ART

THIRTY-FOURTH CENTURY BC

	3400-3376 BC	3375-3351 BC
PEOPLE		
WARS & EVENTS		
DISCOVERIES		
LITERATURE		
MUSIC		
ART		

3350-3326 BC	3325-3301 BC	
		PEOPLE
		WARS & EVENTS
		DISCOVERIES
		LITERATURE
		MUSIC
		ART

THIRTY-THIRD CENTURY BC

	3300-3276 BC	3275-3251 BC
PEOPLE		
WARS & EVENTS		
DISCOVERIES		
LITERATURE		
MUSIC		
ART		

3250-3226 BC	3225-3201 BC	
		PEOPLE
		WARS & EVENTS
		DISCOVERIES
		LITERATURE
		MUSIC
		ART

	3200-3176 BC	3175-3151 BC
PEOPLE		
WARS & EVENTS		
DISCOVERIES		
LITERATURE		
MUSIC		
ART		

3150-3126 BC	3125-3101 BC	
		PEOPLE
		WARS & EVENTS
		DISCOVERIES
		LITERATURE
		MUSIC
		ART

THIRTY-FIRST CENTURY BC

	3100-3076 BC	3075-3051 BC
PEOPLE		
WARS & EVENTS		
DISCOVERIES		
LITERATURE		
MUSIC		
ART		

THIRTY-FIRST CENTURY BC

3050-3026 BC	3025-3001 BC	
		PEOPLE
		WARS & EVENTS
		DISCOVERIES
		LITERATURE
		MUSIC
		ART

THIRTIETH CENTURY BC

	3000-2976 BC	2975-2951 BC
PEOPLE		
WARS & EVENTS		
DISCOVERIES		
LITERATURE		
MUSIC		
ART		

THIRTIETH CENTURY BC

2950-2926 BC	2925-2901 BC	
		PEOPLE
		WARS & EVENTS
		DISCOVERIES
		LITERATURE
		MUSIC
		ART

	2900-2876 BC	2875-2851 BC
PEOPLE		
WARS & EVENTS		
DISCOVERIES		
LITERATURE		
MUSIC		
ART		

2850-2826 BC	2825-2801 BC	
		PEOPLE
		WARS & EVENTS
		DISCOVERIES
		LITERATURE
		MUSIC
		ART

TWENTY-EIGHTH CENTURY BC

	2800-2776 BC	2775-2751 BC
PEOPLE		
WARS & EVENTS		
DISCOVERIES		
LITERATURE		
MUSIC		
ART		

2750-2726 BC	2725-2701 BC	
		PEOPLE
		WARS & EVENTS
		DISCOVERIES
		LITERATURE
		MUSIC
		ART

TWENTY-SEVENTH CENTURY BC

	2700-2676 BC	2675-2651 BC
PEOPLE		
WARS & EVENTS		
DISCOVERIES		
LITERATURE		
MUSIC		
ART		

2650-2626 BC	2625-2601 BC	
		PEOPLE
		WARS & EVENTS
		DISCOVERIES
		LITERATURE
		MUSIC
		ART

TWENTY-SIXTH CENTURY BC

	2600-2576 BC	2575-2551 BC
PEOPLE		
WARS & EVENTS		
DISCOVERIES		
LITERATURE		
MUSIC		
ART		

TWENTY-SIXTH CENTURY BC

2550-2526 BC	2525-2501 BC	
		PEOPLE
		WARS & EVENTS
		DISCOVERIES
		LITERATURE
		MUSIC
		ART

TWENTY-FIFTH CENTURY BC

	2500-2476 BC	2475-2451 BC
PEOPLE		
WARS & EVENTS		
DISCOVERIES		
LITERATURE		
MUSIC		
ART		

TWENTY-FIFTH CENTURY BC

2450-2426 BC	2425-2401 BC	
		PEOPLE
		WARS & EVENTS
		DISCOVERIES
		LITERATURE
		MUSIC
		ART

| 2450-2426 BC | 2425-2401 BC |

TWENTY-FOURTH CENTURY BC

	2400-2376 BC	2375-2351 BC
PEOPLE		
WARS & EVENTS		
DISCOVERIES		
LITERATURE		
MUSIC		
ART		

	2400-2376 BC	2375-2351 BC

2350-2326 BC	2325-2301 BC	
		PEOPLE
		WARS & EVENTS
		DISCOVERIES
		LITERATURE
		MUSIC
		ART

TWENTY-THIRD CENTURY BC

	2300-2276 BC	2275-2251 BC
PEOPLE		
WARS & EVENTS		
DISCOVERIES		
LITERATURE		
MUSIC		
ART		

2250-2226 BC	2225-2201 BC	
		PEOPLE
		WARS & EVENTS
		DISCOVERIES
		LITERATURE
		MUSIC
		ART

TWENTY-SECOND CENTURY BC

	2200-2176 BC	2175-2151 BC
PEOPLE		
WARS & EVENTS		
DISCOVERIES		
LITERATURE		
MUSIC		
ART		

	2200-2176 BC	2175-2151 BC

TWENTY-SECOND CENTURY BC

2150-2126 BC	2125-2101 BC	
		PEOPLE
		WARS & EVENTS
		DISCOVERIES
		LITERATURE
		MUSIC
		ART

TWENTY-FIRST CENTURY BC

	2100-2076 BC	2075-2051 BC
PEOPLE		
WARS & EVENTS		
DISCOVERIES		
LITERATURE		
MUSIC		
ART		

TWENTY-FIRST CENTURY BC

2050-2026 BC	2025-2001 BC	
		PEOPLE
		WARS & EVENTS
		DISCOVERIES
		LITERATURE
		MUSIC
		ART

TWENTIETH CENTURY BC

	2000-1976 BC	1975-1951 BC
PEOPLE		
WARS & EVENTS		
DISCOVERIES		
LITERATURE		
MUSIC		
ART		

TWENTIETH CENTURY BC

1950-1926 BC	1925-1901 BC	
		PEOPLE
		WARS & EVENTS
		DISCOVERIES
		LITERATURE
		MUSIC
		ART

NINETEENTH CENTURY BC

	1900-1876 BC	1875-1851 BC
PEOPLE		
WARS & EVENTS		
DISCOVERIES		
LITERATURE		
MUSIC		
ART		

1850-1826 BC	1825-1801 BC	
		PEOPLE
		WARS & EVENTS
		DISCOVERIES
		LITERATURE
		MUSIC
		ART

EIGHTEENTH CENTURY BC

	1800-1776 BC	1775-1751 BC
PEOPLE		
WARS & EVENTS		
DISCOVERIES		
LITERATURE		
MUSIC		
ART		

1750-1726 BC	1725-1701 BC	
		PEOPLE
		WARS & EVENTS
		DISCOVERIES
		LITERATURE
		MUSIC
		ART

	1700-1676 BC	1675-1651 BC
PEOPLE		
WARS & EVENTS		
DISCOVERIES		
LITERATURE		
MUSIC		
ART		

1650-1626 BC	1625-1601 BC	
		PEOPLE
		WARS & EVENTS
		DISCOVERIES
		LITERATURE
		MUSIC
		ART

SIXTEENTH CENTURY BC

	1600-1576 BC	1575-1551 BC
PEOPLE		
WARS & EVENTS		
DISCOVERIES		
LITERATURE		
MUSIC		
ART		

1550-1526 BC	1525-1501 BC	
		PEOPLE
		WARS & EVENTS
		DISCOVERIES
		LITERATURE
		MUSIC
		ART

FIFTEENTH CENTURY BC

	1500-1476 BC	1475-1451 BC
PEOPLE		
WARS & EVENTS		
DISCOVERIES		
LITERATURE		
MUSIC		
ART		

FIFTEENTH CENTURY BC

1450-1426 BC	1425-1401 BC	
		PEOPLE
		WARS & EVENTS
		DISCOVERIES
		LITERATURE
		MUSIC
		ART

FOURTEENTH CENTURY BC

	1400-1376 BC	1375-1351 BC
PEOPLE		
WARS & EVENTS		
DISCOVERIES		
LITERATURE		
MUSIC		
ART		

	1400-1376 BC	1375-1351 BC

1350-1326 BC	1325-1301 BC	
		PEOPLE
		WARS & EVENTS
		DISCOVERIES
		LITERATURE
		MUSIC
		ART

	1300-1276 BC	1275-1251 BC
PEOPLE		
WARS & EVENTS		
DISCOVERIES		
LITERATURE		
MUSIC		
ART		

1250-1226 BC	1225-1201 BC	
		PEOPLE
		WARS & EVENTS
		DISCOVERIES
		LITERATURE
		MUSIC
		ART

TWELFTH CENTURY BC

	1200-1176 BC	1175-1151 BC
PEOPLE		
WARS & EVENTS		
DISCOVERIES		
LITERATURE		
MUSIC		
ART		

1150-1126 BC	1125-1101 BC	
		PEOPLE
		WARS & EVENTS
		DISCOVERIES
		LITERATURE
		MUSIC
		ART

ELEVENTH CENTURY BC

	1100-1076 BC	1075-1051 BC
PEOPLE		
WARS & EVENTS		
DISCOVERIES		
LITERATURE		
MUSIC		
ART		

ELEVENTH CENTURY BC

1050-1026 BC	1025-1001 BC	
		PEOPLE
		WARS & EVENTS
		DISCOVERIES
		LITERATURE
		MUSIC
		ART

TENTH CENTURY BC

	1000-976 BC	975-951 BC
PEOPLE		
WARS & EVENTS		
DISCOVERIES		
LITERATURE		
MUSIC		
ART		

TENTH CENTURY BC

950-926 BC	925-901 BC	
		PEOPLE
		WARS & EVENTS
		DISCOVERIES
		LITERATURE
		MUSIC
		ART

NINTH CENTURY BC

	900-876 BC	875-851 BC
PEOPLE		
WARS & EVENTS		
DISCOVERIES		
LITERATURE		
MUSIC		
ART		

NINTH CENTURY BC

850-826 BC	825-801 BC	
		PEOPLE
		WARS & EVENTS
		DISCOVERIES
		LITERATURE
		MUSIC
		ART

EIGHTH CENTURY BC

	800-776 BC	775-751 BC
PEOPLE		
WARS & EVENTS		
DISCOVERIES		
LITERATURE		
MUSIC		
ART		

EIGHTH CENTURY BC

750-726 BC	725-701 BC	
		PEOPLE
		WARS & EVENTS
		DISCOVERIES
		LITERATURE
		MUSIC
		ART

SEVENTH CENTURY BC

	700-676 BC	675-651 BC
PEOPLE		
WARS & EVENTS		
DISCOVERIES		
LITERATURE		
MUSIC		
ART		

SEVENTH CENTURY BC

650-626 BC	625-601 BC	
		PEOPLE
		WARS & EVENTS
		DISCOVERIES
		LITERATURE
		MUSIC
		ART

SIXTH CENTURY BC

	600-576 BC	575-551 BC
PEOPLE		
WARS & EVENTS		
DISCOVERIES		
LITERATURE		
MUSIC		
ART		

SIXTH CENTURY BC

550-526 BC	525-501 BC

PEOPLE

WARS & EVENTS

DISCOVERIES

LITERATURE

MUSIC

ART

FIFTH CENTURY BC

	500-476 BC	475-451 BC
PEOPLE		
WARS & EVENTS		
DISCOVERIES		
LITERATURE		
MUSIC		
ART		

FIFTH CENTURY BC

450-426 BC	425-401 BC	
		PEOPLE
		WARS & EVENTS
		DISCOVERIES
		LITERATURE
		MUSIC
		ART

FOURTH CENTURY BC

	400-376 BC	375-351 BC
PEOPLE		
WARS & EVENTS		
DISCOVERIES		
LITERATURE		
MUSIC		
ART		

FOURTH CENTURY BC

350-326 BC	325-301 BC	
		PEOPLE
		WARS & EVENTS
		DISCOVERIES
		LITERATURE
		MUSIC
		ART

THIRD CENTURY BC

	300-276 BC	275-251 BC
PEOPLE		
WARS & EVENTS		
DISCOVERIES		
LITERATURE		
MUSIC		
ART		

250-226 BC	225-201 BC	
		PEOPLE
		WARS & EVENTS
		DISCOVERIES
		LITERATURE
		MUSIC
		ART
250-226 BC	225-201 BC	

SECOND CENTURY BC

	200-176 BC	175-151 BC
PEOPLE		
WARS & EVENTS		
DISCOVERIES		
LITERATURE		
MUSIC		
ART		

SECOND CENTURY BC

150-126 BC	125-101 BC	
		PEOPLE
		WARS & EVENTS
		DISCOVERIES
		LITERATURE
		MUSIC
		ART

	100-76 BC	75-51 BC
PEOPLE		
WARS & EVENTS		
DISCOVERIES		
LITERATURE		
MUSIC		
ART		

50-26 BC	25-1 BC	
		PEOPLE
		WARS & EVENTS
		DISCOVERIES
		LITERATURE
		MUSIC
		ART

FIRST CENTURY AD

	AD 1-25	AD 26-50
PEOPLE		
WARS & EVENTS		
DISCOVERIES		
LITERATURE		
MUSIC		
ART		

FIRST CENTURY AD

AD 51-75	AD 76-100	
		PEOPLE
		WARS & EVENTS
		DISCOVERIES
		LITERATURE
		MUSIC
		ART

SECOND CENTURY AD

	AD 101-125	AD 126-150
PEOPLE		
WARS & EVENTS		
DISCOVERIES		
LITERATURE		
MUSIC		
ART		

AD 151-175	AD 176-200	
		PEOPLE
		WARS & EVENTS
		DISCOVERIES
		LITERATURE
		MUSIC
		ART

THIRD CENTURY AD

	AD 201-225	AD 226-250
PEOPLE		
WARS & EVENTS		
DISCOVERIES		
LITERATURE		
MUSIC		
ART		

THIRD CENTURY AD

AD 251-275	AD 276-300	
		PEOPLE
		WARS & EVENTS
		DISCOVERIES
		LITERATURE
		MUSIC
		ART

FOURTH CENTURY AD

	AD 301-325	AD 326-350
PEOPLE		
WARS & EVENTS		
DISCOVERIES		
LITERATURE		
MUSIC		
ART		

FOURTH CENTURY AD

AD 351-375	AD 376-400	
		PEOPLE
		WARS & EVENTS
		DISCOVERIES
		LITERATURE
		MUSIC
		ART

FIFTH CENTURY AD

AD 401-425	AD 426-450
PEOPLE	
WARS & EVENTS	
DISCOVERIES	
LITERATURE	
MUSIC	
ART	

FIFTH CENTURY AD

AD 451-475	AD 476-500	
		PEOPLE
		WARS & EVENTS
		DISCOVERIES
		LITERATURE
		MUSIC
		ART

SIXTH CENTURY AD

	AD 501-525	AD 526-550
PEOPLE		
WARS & EVENTS		
DISCOVERIES		
LITERATURE		
MUSIC		
ART		

SIXTH CENTURY AD

AD 551-575	AD 576-600	
		PEOPLE
		WARS & EVENTS
		DISCOVERIES
		LITERATURE
		MUSIC
		ART

SEVENTH CENTURY AD

	AD 601-625	AD 626-650
PEOPLE		
WARS & EVENTS		
DISCOVERIES		
LITERATURE		
MUSIC		
ART		

SEVENTH CENTURY AD

AD 651-675	AD 676-700	
		PEOPLE
		WARS & EVENTS
		DISCOVERIES
		LITERATURE
		MUSIC
		ART

EIGHTH CENTURY AD

	AD 701-725	AD 726-750
PEOPLE		
WARS & EVENTS		
DISCOVERIES		
LITERATURE		
MUSIC		
ART		

EIGHTH CENTURY AD

AD 751-775	AD 776-800	
		PEOPLE
		WARS & EVENTS
		DISCOVERIES
		LITERATURE
		MUSIC
		ART

NINTH CENTURY AD

AD 801-825	AD 826-850

PEOPLE

WARS & EVENTS

DISCOVERIES

LITERATURE

MUSIC

ART

NINTH CENTURY AD

AD 851-875	AD 876-900	
		PEOPLE
		WARS & EVENTS
		DISCOVERIES
		LITERATURE
		MUSIC
		ART

TENTH CENTURY AD

	AD 901-925	AD 926-950
PEOPLE		
WARS & EVENTS		
DISCOVERIES		
LITERATURE		
MUSIC		
ART		

TENTH CENTURY AD

AD 951-975	AD 976-1000	
		PEOPLE
		WARS & EVENTS
		DISCOVERIES
		LITERATURE
		MUSIC
		ART

ELEVENTH CENTURY AD

	AD 1001-1025	AD 1026-1050
PEOPLE		
WARS & EVENTS		
DISCOVERIES		
LITERATURE		
MUSIC		
ART		

ELEVENTH CENTURY AD

AD 1051-1075	AD 1076-1100	
		PEOPLE
		WARS & EVENTS
		DISCOVERIES
		LITERATURE
		MUSIC
		ART

TWELFTH CENTURY AD

	AD 1101-1125	AD 1126-1150
PEOPLE		
WARS & EVENTS		
DISCOVERIES		
LITERATURE		
MUSIC		
ART		

TWELFTH CENTURY AD

AD 1151-1175	AD 1176-1200	
		PEOPLE
		WARS & EVENTS
		DISCOVERIES
		LITERATURE
		MUSIC
		ART

THIRTEENTH CENTURY AD

AD 1201-1225	AD 1226-1250
PEOPLE	
WARS & EVENTS	
DISCOVERIES	
LITERATURE	
MUSIC	
ART	

THIRTEENTH CENTURY AD

AD 1251-1275	AD 1276-1300	
		PEOPLE
		WARS & EVENTS
		DISCOVERIES
		LITERATURE
		MUSIC
		ART

FOURTEENTH CENTURY AD

	AD 1301-1325	AD 1326-1350
PEOPLE		
WARS & EVENTS		
DISCOVERIES		
LITERATURE		
MUSIC		
ART		

FOURTEENTH CENTURY AD

AD 1351-1375	AD 1376-1400	
		PEOPLE
		WARS & EVENTS
		DISCOVERIES
		LITERATURE
		MUSIC
		ART

FIFTEENTH CENTURY AD

	AD 1401-1425	AD 1426-1450
PEOPLE		
WARS & EVENTS		
DISCOVERIES		
LITERATURE		
MUSIC		
ART		

FIFTEENTH CENTURY AD

AD 1451-1475	AD 1476-1500	
		PEOPLE
		WARS & EVENTS
		DISCOVERIES
		LITERATURE
		MUSIC
		ART

SIXTEENTH CENTURY AD

	AD 1501-1525	AD 1526-1550
PEOPLE		
WARS & EVENTS		
DISCOVERIES		
LITERATURE		
MUSIC		
ART		

SIXTEENTH CENTURY AD

AD 1551-1575	AD 1576-1600	
		PEOPLE
		WARS & EVENTS
		DISCOVERIES
		LITERATURE
		MUSIC
		ART

SEVENTEENTH CENTURY AD

	AD 1601-1625	AD 1626-1650
PEOPLE		
WARS & EVENTS		
DISCOVERIES		
LITERATURE		
MUSIC		
ART		

SEVENTEENTH CENTURY AD

AD 1651-1675	AD 1676-1700	
		PEOPLE
		WARS & EVENTS
		DISCOVERIES
		LITERATURE
		MUSIC
		ART

EIGHTEENTH CENTURY AD

	AD 1701-1725	AD 1726-1750
PEOPLE		
WARS & EVENTS		
DISCOVERIES		
LITERATURE		
MUSIC		
ART		

EIGHTEENTH CENTURY AD

AD 1751-1775	AD 1776-1800	
		PEOPLE
		WARS & EVENTS
		DISCOVERIES
		LITERATURE
		MUSIC
		ART

NINETEENTH CENTURY AD

	AD 1801-1825	AD 1826-1850
PEOPLE		
WARS & EVENTS		
DISCOVERIES		
LITERATURE		
MUSIC		
ART		

NINETEENTH CENTURY AD

AD 1851-1875	AD 1876-1900	
		PEOPLE
		WARS & EVENTS
		DISCOVERIES
		LITERATURE
		MUSIC
		ART

TWENTIETH CENTURY AD

	AD 1901-1925	AD 1926-1950
PEOPLE		
WARS & EVENTS		
DISCOVERIES		
LITERATURE		
MUSIC		
ART		

TWENTIETH CENTURY AD

AD 1951-1975	AD 1976-2000	
		PEOPLE
		WARS & EVENTS
		DISCOVERIES
		LITERATURE
		MUSIC
		ART

TWENTY-FIRST CENTURY AD

	AD 2001-2025	AD 2026-2050
PEOPLE		
WARS & EVENTS		
DISCOVERIES		
LITERATURE		
MUSIC		
ART		

TWENTY-FIRST CENTURY AD

AD 2051-2075	AD 2076-2100

PEOPLE

WARS & EVENTS

DISCOVERIES

LITERATURE

MUSIC

ART

DRAWINGS

NOTES

DRAWINGS

NOTES

DRAWINGS

NOTES

DRAWINGS

NOTES

Made in United States
Troutdale, OR
02/15/2024